The Sharing Journal

A Guide to

Better Communication

Alexa Grace Simmons

ISBN: 9781540827616
Published
Printed in the United States of America

Dedication

This book is dedicated to my children. They are and will forever be my greatest love in life. They make me proud every day and I have been so fortunate to have such a great relationship with them both. I have spent my life encouraging their dreams, and now they are encouraging mine. I am blessed. And to my husband who always supports me, loves me, and never tries to change me.

Introduction

This book is intended to be a conversation starter of sorts. A bunch of simple fun questions about yourself, the person you care about and your relationship, thrown in with much more in depth ones. I like to mix it up a bit so the questions are in no particular order. The answers given are meant to be short but are the beginning of dialogue pertaining to the question. Maybe there are things you are not comfortable talking about but you feel you need to. Maybe there are certain things you wish your partner would ask you about but doesn't and you are not sure how to tell them.

Maybe they have hurt your feelings without even knowing it and you want to start a conversation about it. This book is a guide to better communication and emotional intimacy. You will also find that it will help you discover and rediscover things about yourself, your inner most thoughts, wishes and dreams.

The books can be used individually or together. You can fill out your own book and give it to the person you care about or you can go through the pages together and at a certain point swap books to read each other's answers and take time to reflect on them. That should really help lead you toward good constructive open and loving dialogue.

About Me

I am writing this book as a tool for those of you out there who are like me. I am someone who if you get me mad I can tell you exactly what I am thinking, every single thought and emotion I am having, no holds barred. However, if you hurt my feelings I go completely the opposite way. I shut down, withdraw and cannot find the words needed to express how I feel, I keep it all in. Although you may pick up that there is an issue, I will not tell you what it is.

I am someone who does not like feeling vulnerable in any way, especially emotionally. If someone hurts my feelings I become very quiet and am just slowly working through it all in my own mind and heart.

To be truly open and honest in a relationship you have to be able to express hurt constructively, to let the other person know how they have hurt you. Hopefully in doing so they will apologize, you work through it and you learn and grow together. This applies to any relationship, significant other, son, daughter, mother, father, and friend, whoever is important in your life.

Emotional health in my opinion is the most important kind of health. Hold on to it, nurture and protect it. Always be true to yourself, be honest and live from the heart.

All relationships teach us something about ourselves. What we need, what we will accept and how we treat others. I love to watch the evolution of various relationships in my life and take the lessons that are presented. Cherish them all...good and bad, as they give us a chance to grow.

In life we are always communicating in one way or another and typically multiple ways at the same time with both verbal and nonverbal cues. Life in the simplest form is about communicating and connecting with people in the best way possible. The more you know and understand yourself the more effectively you can communicate with others. Have fun with this book and take time to really reflect on it.

Forward

by Gina Crawford

When my dearest friend asked me to take a look at a book idea she was working on, I was a little apprehensive because not only did I not have time; I don't read much and I am not into "self-help" type books. I reluctantly agreed because she has and will do anything for anyone AND is the pillar of strength and wisdom.

When I started reading the draft transcript of this journal, I can honestly and literally say, "She had me at hello". I was instantly engaged and overwhelmed with how perfect and relevant this journal was for all aspects of life. It is simple, yet fun and retrospective – which for me was perfect. The journal is an "adult mad lib" but with a purpose. I truly felt like the journal was designed specifically for me (but it will undoubtedly make everyone feel that way).

This Sharing Journal is perfect if you want to get to know yourself again (sometimes that can be lost in this thing called life). It is perfect to ignite a spark in your relationship and get to know each other again —especially in a situation where you realize the person you married is not the same person 20 years later. It is fun for new relationships, and an effective communication tool in any relationship. Essentially — it is perfect for you to find out who you are and other's to find out who you are (and vice versa) which leads to more fulfilling and happy relationships and life. Take a break from your hectic routine and leap into this Sharing Journal —you will not regret it.

My middle name

My favorite color (s)

My favorite meal (s)

My favorite dessert (s)

My favorite time of day

My favorite earliest childhood memory

My first pet was

My favorite memory of my pet was

School to me was

High school to me was

First real boyfriend / girlfriend was

That relationship was good in the following ways

That relationship was bad in the following ways

What I learned from that relationship

What I should have learned

The overall theme of my childhood was

If I had to describe my relationship with my mother/mother figure in my life in 3 words I would say (with explanation)

If I had to describe my relationship with my father/father figure in my life in 3 words I would say (with explanation)

My siblings are

My relationship with them (him or her) growing up was

Now it is

Because

My relationship with my mother has changed over the years

because

My relationship with my father has changed over the years be-cause

The best thing I learned from my parents

The worst thing I learned from my parents

The one relative I wish I could trade in is

Because

Best high school memory

Worst high school memory

Favorite year of High School

What lessons I learned from High School

The one thing I have never told anyone about high school is

The most spontaneous thing I regret doing is

The most spontaneous thing I will never regret

I feel most confident about myself when

The most confident time in my life was / is

When I think I lost my confidence

Because

I am most easily hurt when / by

The people in my life who hurt me the most are

How I let them hurt me

Why I continue to let it happen

Ways you can help me

I enjoy our relationship so much because

When I am with you I typically feel

I need you to   more

I need you to   less

I am most self-conscious about (part of your body)

Because

I am most proud of (this body part)

Because

Something (s) that you do that you think is funny but I do not

Because

Something (s) that you do that I think is hilarious and you don't even realize it

Something that you always say that hurts my feelings

My secret wish for my life is

If I could choose a different career it would be

Because

If I had a "do over" I would

Something that has happened to me that I have never talked about but really need to

Favorite rainy Sunday activities

Favorite season (s)

Because

In the winter, all I want to do is

Top 5 favorite things I like to do in the summer

You make me laugh the most when

Something(s) you never knew about me

The things I admire most about you

When I am mad I

When I am sad I

I am happiest when

Someday soon can we find time to

Your friends make me feel

Sometimes you seem different when

The 5 best words that I would use to describe myself are

The 5 best words I would use to describe you are

The 5 best words that describe our relationship

I feel most secure when

I love the way you make me feel when

The parts of myself that I would like to work on

The thing(s) I love most about myself

The things I love most about you

The things I love most about the two of us together

My favorite way to recharge is

My goals for our relationship are

My favorite thing (s) about you

The thing(s) you say or do that maybe isn't (aren't) my favorite thing(s)

Because

I was/am the most proud of you when

Farthest I have ever traveled

Some of our funniest moments so far

Some of our best moments so far

If we could go on a dream vacation I would you like to go

My guess is that you would like to go to

The last place I would ever go on vacation

The best compliment (s) you have ever given me

My favorite movie (s) of all time

Favorite book(s)

Favorite city

My favorite memory of us is

What I have learned from our relationship

What I hope you have learned from me thus far

I am the worst at

I am the best at

If I had a super power(s) it/they would be

How I would use my super powers

My favorite memory as a child

My worst memory as child

Something(s) I truly believe in that makes no sense at all

My favorite bad for you cheat food(s)

If I won the lottery the first 10 things I would do

Top 10 things on my Bucket List

Something that someone told me that I have never shared with anyone

The sound that makes me the happiest

The sound that annoys me the most

Favorite saying(s)

Favorite holiday(s)

If I could wear   every day I would

If I could eat   every day I would

My secret wish for you is

My secret wish for myself

My favorite thing(s) to do on a car ride

My favorite way(s) to destress

Favorite thing to do when I have the house to myself

The main reason I stay at my job is

If I could have a day full of all of my favorite things it would consist of

One place we have gone that I will never return to

Because

My favorite place(s) we have gone together

Because

My favorite place that you have not yet been to is

I love it when you

If I could choose a new career for you it would be

Because

We need more   in our days

We need less   in our days

My deepest fear about life is

My deepest fear about our relationship is

If you could pick a new career for me what would it be

Because

If I could change something about you, it would be

Because

Thank you for never

You are the best at reminding me to

I would like our relationship to improve in the following ways

My worst habit is

One of the best and most unexpected things that ever has

ever happened to me

If I didn't have to worry about money I would

Something I should have said to you a long time ago

Something I said that I never should have

I am sorry for

Dream(s) I wish I had never given up on

Goals that I am making for myself

The worst thing that you have said that I am having trouble let-
ting go of

Sometimes you hurt me and don't even realize it....some examples are

I am sorry if I hurt you when

If I could make up for it in anyway what would it be?

The most hurtful words from you are when you say

I need to feel like more a priority than

When you say   I hear

Growing up I always wanted to be

Three traditions from my childhood that I would like to pass on

The things you do that make me feel insecure

The things you do that make me feel secure

My very first impression of you was

I really liked the way you

My overall philosophy in life is

I think at least one day a week we should

The best gift you ever gave me was

The gift (s) that made me go hmmmmmm?

5 ways that we are different

5 ways we are exactly the same

Let's start each day with

Let's end the day with

I fell in love with you because

Instead of saying   try saying

Thank you for always

I wish we had never

The best thing(s) you can do for me if I am sad

The best thing(s) you can do for me if I am mad

My earliest memory or us

Some of the funniest things you have ever said that still crack me up today

The one sport I should never attempt

Something you believe about me that may not quite be true..

The best advice anyone has ever given me

The advice I would give my younger self

What I love about our relationship is

The greatest gift life has given me so far

The best ways I have changed over the years

The ways I wish I hadn't changed over the years

My favorite ways you have changed

My favorite ways you have stayed the same

My vision for the future personally and professionally is

I appreciate they way you have brought out these elements of my personality

The greatest life lessons I have learned so far

Do you remember the time we....

I wish we talked more about

Let' make plans to

I really appreciate that you notice

My favorite dish that you make is

My least favorite dish is

I want us to spend more time with

I think we could spend less time with

You make me so proud when

I knew we were perfect for each other when

I did have some doubts when

I am glad we made it through

Everyday is a good day with you because

I think overall our communication is

I wish we had communicated more before deciding

I wish we were more expressive in the following ways

When we were first together I thought

Little did I know

The best examples of how well we work together

The best examples of how we need to improve

I have noticed to following patterns in our relationship that are good

I have noticed the following patterns that I would like to work on

I am thankful for the following pattern in our relationship

The best habit we do together is

The worst habit we have gotten in to

A habit I would like us to get into

A habit we need to break as soon as possible

I see us spending our retirement

5 Things in life I wish I would have figured out sooner

5 Things in life I am glad I figured out later

If I had a regret in life it would be

I am so glad I never

I am so glad I decided to

5 Things I would never change about you

This summer let's plan to

This fall let's plan to

This spring let's plan to

I am grateful for you because

I am so proud of myself for overcoming

I am so proud of you for overcoming

My best strength is

My weakness is

Your best strength is

Your weakness is

Our greatest strength is

I think most people think we are

But really we are

I wish we were

I am really glad we are not

I will always cherish our relationship because

I hope that you have learned from me

I know that I have learned the following from you

If there is any doubt that I love you with all of my heart I would like to say the following to let you know and thank you for our journey thus far.....

I hope that you use the last pages for your own words...your own conversation starters or things that help truly reveal yourself to the ones you care most about and yourself.

Good communication is an essential part of any great relationship in life....

Never be afraid to express your thoughts and emotions..

Be true to yourself

Love who you are....

Own who you are....

Share your genuine self....always

Life is meant to be full of love and laughter to be shared with those we love....

Stay true to your heart....

Your heart is much smarter than your brain....

Life is short....use your time wisely....

Please send me your thoughts about the book at

alexagsimmons@gmail.com

31390791R00057

Made in the USA
Middletown, DE
06 January 2019